Life In a Jar
Living with Dyslexia and Dyspraxia

Stephen Sutton

authorHOUSE®

AuthorHouse™ UK
1663 Liberty Drive
Bloomington, IN 47403 USA
www.authorhouse.co.uk
Phone: UK TFN: 0800 0148641 (Toll Free inside the UK)
*   UK Local: (02) 0369 56322 (+44 20 3695 6322 from outside the UK)*

Published by AuthorHouse 04/01/2022

ISBN: 978-1-4208-4210-4 (sc)

Print information available on the last page.

LIFE IN A JAR

INTRODUCTION

This title is ambiguous because it has more than one meaning, the jar can be a form of protection from the outside world, a way of keeping people or thoughts out .Or a prison that traps its victim restricting the person and subjecting them to a life of misery . Many problems could be said to be related to these conditions physical illness such as Asthma,angina or other related health problems . Or Dyslexia affecting the academic side reading, writing etc.. ... Whatever the problem is, it causes many problems in living a normal every day existence. People therefore become isolate alienated from the world, confused wondering whom to turn to for help. This is the reason that I have written this in the hope to point the way to help others to find the help they need and live life to the full.

Life in a jar represents the restrictive and protective aspects of our lives, the subjects age and gender in the jar is irrelevant, the main feature is the object e.g. the jar and what it represents to the individual this inanimate object could just as easily be a gold fish bowl or fish tank, a cage or transparent box. Whoever you are you could live in a jar, at some point in our lives we become that person within the jar, lonely, naked and vulnerable. However some of us like the thought of being inside the jar, as a form of protection, the jar becomes our womb our very existence is protected, sustained, fed and nourished within and cut off from the outside world.

Alternatively being imprisoned means not being able to do as we please, restricted with no definite direction to go in, no guidance and feeling uncontrollably helpless like floating around in a weightless room. The subject or victim wants to break out but they have no means of escape many people can be in this predicament are you one of them? Do you suffer from abuse, asthma, dyslexia, school bullying, a victim of crime, or live on the streets as one of the homeless consider the situations the many illnesses that disable people or are the cause of mental illness do you live in a jar. Try to form your own definition of life in a jar while you enjoy reading this book and if you have a story to tell please write to me at email –steversutton@hotmail.co.uk

Life in a jar is by no means intended to be an educational publication, rather it aims to become a source of encouragement and provide readers with positive thoughts regarding their predicament. The need to do this came from the author's observations and personal experience of life in various predicaments. Indeed the authors own life story gave him the main driving force for doing something positive for society on an international level. Needless to say the author requires a great deal of co-operation from the public in which to achieve his objectives. Peoples own life stories of courage and determination to reach their goal form the body of this book. I wrote this book and had it published in 2005, however I found it necessary to make a few alterations and republished it in 2020. During editing the book my friend Richard Howarth passed away October 2019 he is featured in this book going back to my school days.

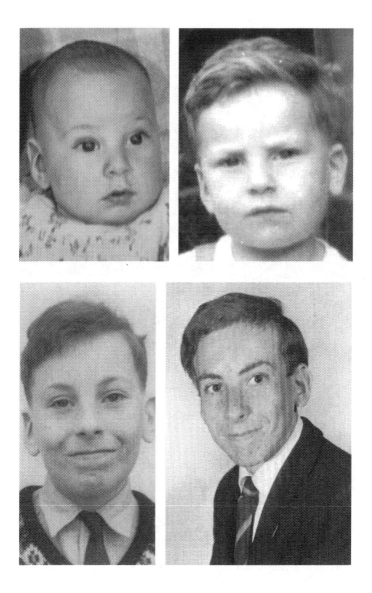

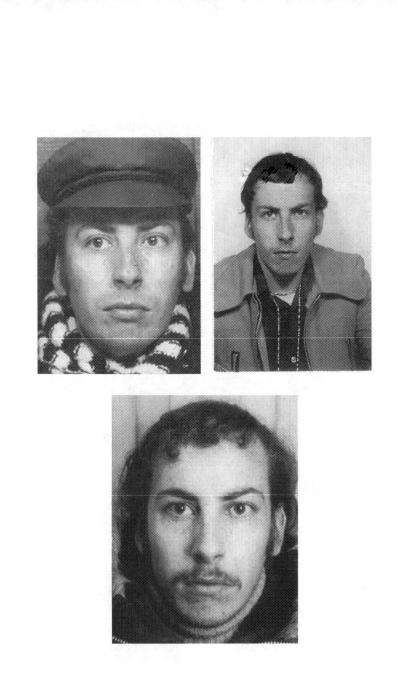

CONTENTS

LIVING WITH DYSLEXIA

My own life in a jar involves being born with dyslexia, diagnosed as asthmatic, abuse mentally and physically at school, bullied, attempted suicide at sixteen, raped at sixteen, blind at eighteen (my sight is back now of course), suffered from depression at thirty-two and suffering from stress at forty-four, my life has been turbulent and all recorded in this book. Throughout this book I shall be discussing the highs and lows of living with dyslexia. The purpose of which will explain why people live in a jar, either becoming trapped or protected by having a false sense of security.

Being born with dyslexia and struggling through school and work made me realise that life was a continual battle of survival, but I was determined to live as normal a life as possible, also having asthma allowed me to empathise with other sufferers, one problem after another seemed to hound my teenage years, I experienced a number of traumatic events some were linked to dyslexia. In my twenties and early thirties, I experienced life in many ways, travelling around the world certainly broadened my horizons. Having a taste of other people way of life made me more aware of the many problems that occur in the world, and how disabilities, abuse, bullying, and racism are indeed world-wide problems.

In my late thirties and early forties my life changed dramatically. I met my wife in Blackpool, we lived together for a while, and then we got married. We had four children my career took off and I am now looking back at my days at university thinking how on earth did I graduate with so many problems to contend with. Now I am a qualified nurse with qualifications that I never thought I would get. I suffered from stress, but with help

from my wife Jayne, children, friends, G.P and a nice councillor called Michelle I managed to bounce back to health. It was during my sessions with Michelle that caused me to reflect on my life, and see the achievements that I had made against all odds. This gave me the idea of sharing my experiences with others in the hope that people may benefit by my example, and strive forward to meet their goal. Also, by seeing other people's examples of survival and success in similar situations or even in worse environments, life in a jar opens the lid from many peoples lives, allowing their truth to escape and providing them with the freedom to be as free of the jar, as I finally am.

THIS BOOK

This book highlights problems associated with dyslexia, such as poor concentration, short term memory deficit, clumsiness, and in some cases optical problems such as Scotopic sensitivity syndrome.

The author looks back at school life in the sixties and early seventies which involved corporal punishment.

The author also introduces stars who have also told their own story of dyslexia,

And demonstrate how they have survived.

It also looks at possible treatments provided by Brightstar and the DDAT with case studies from various locations.

The author describes the prison system and dyslexia, showing how prison life is changing to accommodate people with learning difficulties.

LIFE IN A JAR

LIVING WITH DYSLEXIA

FACING THE FACTS

The term dyslexia originate from the Greek language, which translated literary means difficulty with (dys) words (lexis). Dyslexia can be divided into many categories each aspect describes a particular problem that the dyslexic may have. For instance, Dysgraphia is a specific difficulty with handwriting, Dysorthographia specific difficulty with spelling, Dyscalculia specific difficulty in numeracy, and Dyspraxia specific difficulties in organisation both of fine and gross motor movement, thinking and perception.

Many successful stories can be told about a condition that I never thought existed called dyslexia. Dyslexia is as real as you and I, however no one knows for certain what truly causes it. There are a few theories based on recent study that seem to lead to the answer.

GENETIC FACTORS

Various researchers have looked at a genetic basis for dyslexia. Researchers have focused on the heredability of reading sub-skills and gene markers of dyslexia on particular chromosomes, 50% is said to be inherited.

Some early research involved post mortem examinations revealing a difference in the structure of dyslexic brains and normal brains, Furthermore new technologies such as Positron Emission Tomography(PET) and Magnetic Resonance Imaging (MRI) have allowed researchers to identify differences in the structure or dysfunction in the Cerebellum (The 'hind brain' thought to be responsible for dexterity and automaticity) offers an explanation for all the manifestations of dyslexia. It affects the speech processing and the motor control processes including time estimation and balance. It is also interesting that information from the language area of the brain and the magnocellular region of the brain is processed through the cerebellum, the weaknesses may well account for the various types of and degrees of dyslexia.

There are more males than females affected, and a high number of the percentages are dyspraxic.

MAGNOCELLULAR/TRANSIENT SYSTEMS

Another theory involves the impaired development of a system of large neurones in the brain (Magnocells) responsible for timing sensory and motor events. The visual demands of reading draw on the magnocellular system and any weakness can lead to visual confusion of letter order and poor visual memory for written word. It is thought that there may also be an auditory equivalent that is essential for meeting the phonological demands of reading. This can cause a weakness leading to difficulties such as the confusion of letter sounds.

A COMMON PROBLEM

Many people are said to be suffering from dyslexia, famous people such as Winston Churchill, Albert Einstein, Sylvester Stallone, Tom Cruise, Duncan Goodhew, and

John Craven. In fact 4-5% of the population of Britain are dyslexic two million of these are severely dyslexic, some people are not even noticed, they hide their condition in shame as if its there own fault. Dyslexia is a form of word blindness, or number blindness, but the definition means much more than this. The dyslexic Institute describes it as ' Organising or learning difficulties which restrict the student's competencies in information processing, in motor skills and working memory, so causing limitations in some or all of the skills of speech, reading, spelling, hand writing, essay writing, numeracy and behaviour '. (Dyslexic institute 1989)

The British dyslexia association (B. D. A) Describes Dyslexia as ' A specific difficulty in learning, constitutional in origin, in one or more of reading spelling and written language which may be accompanied by number work. It is particularly related to mastering and using written language (alphabet, numerical and musical notation) although often affecting oral language to some degree '. (British dyslexia association 1989) One of the problems I find, as a dyslexic is that, words can merge into one confusing muddle of non-sensible mess. Short-term memory problems cause a failure to retain information, and from the writing aspect the brain races on much faster than the hand the words then get jumbled up. This results in frustration embarrassment because other people then read your work and laugh at your spelling mistakes.

LIFE IN A JAR

LIVING WITH DYSLEXIA

MY SCHOOL DAYS

Many stories are told about people living with dyslexia, coping with their condition, some people reach high positions in good jobs; others develop into university students and find themselves in good careers. My own story was one of success though I struggled to get there, I was determined to get there to reach my goal. This is how I did it.

At the age of four, I began school at the Willows infant school. This lasted a short period until a new school was built and I was moved to Chadsmead Infant School. Chadsmead was divided into two schools' infants and juniors. I was in a class where a teacher used to shout at the children, my mother said she must have hated children, especially clumsy, thick children like me. She must have thought she was in a class for the deaf; I have always been sensitive to loud noise. It was probably at this point that my Asthma started; I did lose a lot of schooling through my health. It was considered that my Asthma was triggered off by childhood stress, which could have been induced by anxiety. I remember painting pictures of roman soldiers and drawing in books. I was particularly keen on art; this was because it was something that I was able to do. Thinking back, it was also therapeutic, and helped me relax and forget my stresses. I always considered punishment at school an unnecessary act of cruelty and humiliation. Some teachers actually seemed to thrive on hitting children, this type of punishment was said to be affective for some, but caused anxiety to others. All it did for me was to cause an asthma attack. One of the most humiliating experiences in early school life was being sent to the headmistress to be punished, she would put children over her knee and slap their legs. Other children used to watch this event through the window and laugh.

During my times off school with asthma, I utilised my hours by reading comics, I discovered by looking at the actions on the comic strips that I was able to interpret what was being said. Most of the cartoons were drawn in a systematic way; this made life easy for me trying to follow the story line. I could decipher what was being said by the actions of the people and their expressions.

This was easier than trying to fathom out Janet and John books. This is probably why I spell some words the American way, from mad magazines, and other well-known brands of magazines. English comics included the Beano or Dandy, and later the Eagle.

At the age of seven, I was aware that I had a major problem with reading, writing and retaining information, my father was keen on educating us and was keen on us learning and striving in education, he was a very clever man who I miss so much. Today I dream of him when I need advice and he is always there for me, with a cheery smile and with his pipe sticking out the side of his mouth. My father was a conscientious man, very hard working and would be inclined to give his family his last penny even misses a meal for his children to eat. He was also a very intelligent man who never had the chance to go to university and follow his dream to become a surgeon, as he would have liked. Instead, he was determined to help his three sons' education and teach us at home in order to give us the opportunity that he never had. Although I understand this now, at the time it seemed as if he was just being strict and not appreciating what I was going through. I would sit for long periods of time looking at my shoes trying to figure out left from right, father tried to teach me to tie my shoelaces, but I couldn't remember the sequence. What a dilemma two ways to go and I would choose the wrong one, its a good job there was only a choice of two. Eventually my Aunty Penny taught me, she was left-handed so being ambidextrous I learned to tie them left-handed. I tried to teach my granddaughter left-handed, but she was right-handed.

Junior school was no better, I was placed in a remedial class in a mobile building separate from the rest of the school, and told to copy the writing on a portable black board that rolled, the words seemed to merge and not make sense but I copied them slowly. I was that slow that I used to have to go behind the blackboard and copy the writing upside down when the teacher rolled it rounds. Its no wonder I can now think better standing on my head. Teachers used to hit me and shout if I forgot something such as my dinner money. I was repeatedly hit on the head or had my hands slapped with a ruler. My mother used to send me to the shops for a few items, but if I had no list, I would forget what I was sent for. Not wanting to displease her, I would buy the closest thing as far as I could remember about the product beans instead of peas was a classic. Often, I was sent back to the shop, I tried to concentrate on what was said but still came home with potatoes instead of carrots, or beans instead of peas. I even took a note but couldn't read it, shop keepers would take it off me and read it out which was embarrassing. The worst part of dyslexia is being shown up, best part is creativity.

At this point dyslexia were not even considered as a problem, and certainly not recognised as such, therefore no one could say he's got dyslexia and pinpoint the underlining factors that would indicate that I was suffering from this problem. Both my brothers excelled in what they wanted to do, my older brother always wanted to be a policeman ever since he ran away from home and found himself at a near by police station. My younger brother Andrew was credited to be bright and eager to learn, and so he was encouraged to progress Father seemed so proud of him, though he never mentioned it, he was not noted to vent his feeling, he either kept a lot to himself or conversed to us through my mother. Mother was the mediator, peacekeeper and tended to calm the rough seas. When my mother went into hospital for a while, I felt lost and helpless my Nan looked after us and a Aunty who was only three years older than me, but who made a big impact on my life, because she taught me an easy way to tell the time.

My father tried to teach us maths such as times tables, and how to tell the time. My elder brother Jim was able to take in knowledge quickly, which made me feel frustrated not being able to keep up and caused more pressure on me, he taught me how to draw pencil sketches and make them come to life, art was in the family from my father down to us boys. I tried hard but could never retain information except when my brother showed me by drawing, visual demonstrations were easier for me. My aunty Penny who is four years older than me, discovered that I was ten and not able to tell the time, despite my father and the school trying to help me. She showed me a cake and divided it in half then into quarters etc then she said imagine this is a clock, she explained the meaning of the big hand then the small hand. I was then able to understand and I could actually tell the time.

MY BEST FRIEND RICHARD HOWARTH

I was introduced to Richard in remedial class by Mrs Coalman, she asked me to look after Richard and he sat next to me during this lesson. From that day until we were fourteen years old, we became best friends and were inseparable. We shared our problems of school life and acted out heroes from television in the playground 'The man from UNCLE' was a favourite of ours I was Napoleon Solo and Richard was Illya Kuryakin. We also liked the Monkees TV series and Thunderbirds. We did what children do today exchange cards of TV programs; this was one of the few times that we met children from other classes in their playground. We were socially isolated by from other children by the school system. We were the lepers in the remedial colony, who only met other children by chance. The teachers were in full control of their own curriculum and exercised their discipline as they wished. It was up to Richard and myself to formulate a strategy of survival, we had conjured up a fantasy world like our playground games to counteract the blows indestructible beings like Captain Scarlet or Superman worked quite effectively. This system continued into Comprehensive school until Richards's departure in 1970.

Richard has remained a friend though we parted in 1970 when he moved to Wales I visited once, then lost touch for a while. Then in 1980s I managed to locate him in Yorkshire we sent each other Christmas cards then spoke on the phone a few times in the 1990s. Finally on 20th November 2004 we met again after 33 years both older but still close friends it was as if we had never parted.

Although I had friends I enjoyed my own company, and often played with small plastic toy soldiers. I continued to act this way into adulthood by going for long walks, or travelling alone to places in this country or around the world. When I reached twelve years old, I went to senior school, a comprehensive school with high standards, I was placed in a reading group and the teacher said "Why are you here you can read? "I was not quite sure how to reply to her; yes, I could read but is that the point, was that the only problem I had? No of course not, but I carried on through school regardless struggling through my mock exams and got low grades.

Miss Caines helped me to appreciate poetry, she was my English teacher and librarian at Netherstowe school, she would probably have liked my poetry from 1988 onwards and would have had a copy of my book of poems.

One teacher recognised that I had a problem; Miss Kilby offered to teach me after school so that I could improve. My friends used to think that she had an ulterior motive and teased me about these sessions. I foolishly listened to them, stopped going to her and just managed to pass my C.S.Es in 1972. I even had an IQ test at school, I was asked to read a story and relate it back to the examiner. I was unable to remember a single word and could not describe any of the pictures I saw; this showed I had a short-term memory problem. I read badly and seemed to fail all the tests, due to poor concentration and anxiety.

Miss Kilby won my vote as a good teacher when she took us out as a class and we all entered a café in Lichfield drinking pop and playing the jukebox hits of the time (1969) including Roger Whittaker's Durham town. She got in trouble for us returning back to school late, though we pointed out it was our fault. She kept me after school and helped me with my English literature, I remember her reading 'Loneliness of the long distant runner' by Alan Sillitoe.

At seventeen my school life was finally over; I had survived but received no medals for bravery. I had a private ceremony by a pool, by ripping up my textbooks and casting them vigorously into the water. Goodbye Netherstowe I said to myself I am free from being bullied, ridiculed and tormented. One friend Keith Taylor once said if you could survive school you can cope with anything, this statement remained with me to this day. I kept a library book which Miss Caines kept asking me for called Charles the first, I still have this book to this day. She was another teacher I respected as another English teacher of mine and one who helped me respect poetry, since this time I have published five books of poetry.

On reflection school was not that bad, I had some good times. I liked cooking, art and anything creative. We had a nice art and pottery room combined and a separate art room along the corridor. I remember drawing and painting while listening to music such as Simon and Garfunkel, one art teacher used to let us hear the chart hits of the time. 1971 was a particularly memorable year, the song seemed to express the way I felt at the time Songs like John Kongos 'He's gonna step on you again' reminds me of school bullying Jonathon Kings 'Lazy bones' the laid-back aspect of myself. Tammy Lynn 'I'm gonna run away from you' getting away from school. Greyhounds 'Black and white' about living in racial harmony. And White plain 'When you are a king' being king for a day. It seemed such an emotional time for me, felt so confused, frustrated, angry anxious and in some cases isolated but never knew why.

LIFE IN A JAR

LIVING WITH DYSLEXIA

WORKING DAYS

My next course of action was college on a pre-nursing course, my father had his doubts about me coping with such a course if I struggled at school surely, I would find it difficult at college. However, I tried and failed he was right I found the course work impossible and the tutors very unhelpful and frankly sometimes rude. I therefore went to work I tried printing and found myself printing hospital forms to my irony, then I tried woodwork, engineering, farming, shop work and hotel work, but still met problems with dyslexia, I was in a dilemma like a non- stop carousel ride going no where. One of the symptoms of dyslexia/dyspraxia was clumsiness and was I clumsy, I was and still am a walking hazard or an accident waiting to happen. People used to see me in plaster or with an arm in a sling and say "Have an accident? "In which I replied "No thanks I have just had one ". No wonder I became unemployable, I was a walking liability. One employer asked how could have so many accidents in one day? I replied it's easy I get up early. Even back at school I remember falling through a set of doors damaging my head, or running away from a caretaker tripping and breaking my arm. Infact it was that bad at school that the hospital used to save me a bed for my next visit.

I had been in many places, worked in all sorts of environments, from farms, shops, factories to hotels, leaving devastation behind me, twenty jobs by the age of twenty. Not that I'm proud of this, but it is relevant to mention in order to put the story straight. At twenty-three I'd been at a re-establishment centre organised by the D.H.S.S In order to get me into the routine of work, which was likened by some people to an open prison (with a few strange characters), I spent my time gardening and cleaning the dormitories. Then I got a job in Stratford upon Avon in a hotel and left soon afterwards (probably after knocking a waiter out when I went through the wrong revolving door, he was carrying a series of dishes and delicious trifles. I was then sent to a rehabilitation centre in Coventry to assess what type of work suited me, they suggested clerical work, which I was neither qualified for or could cope with effectively. At seventeen I was raped in London which caused me to have night terrors, I never told anybody until I reached thirty something happened to bring the whole nasty experience flooding back in my mind. I became suicidal by then. I took an overdose at Seventeen following my ordeal in London once again my older brother was at my side helping me, he escorted me in the ambulance when I went to have my stomach pumped. He offered support and advice; I can honestly say he saved my life. He asked me why I had done it, I said it was over a girl I had been with called Sandra, her father split us up. In truth it was more than that, the rape incident by two men had devastated me, I had been picked up at a London train station and taken to this apartment somewhere in London. The whole purpose was the abduction and rape, I feared for my life and fortunately the only kept me twenty-four hours realising I was under eighty they let me go. I blamed myself for getting myself in to the situation, but in reality, it was those perverts lingering at the station waiting for teenagers. It probably still happens where they talk to you lull you into a false sense of security and take you off to use you for sex or worse. I never told anybody about the assault until at least fifteen years later, I was too ashamed of myself and as I previously said guilty as well as dirty and defiled. I had night terrors, reliving the event over and over, nightmares punished me and nobody knew. I finally told my mother when aids came about, hoping that I wasn't HIV positive, which would have been a new scare for me.

I eventually managed to get a job where my mother had once worked, at a residential home for the elderly at Nearfield house. I really enjoyed the work it was so good to help the elderly so rewarding though my clumsiness continued and seemed to get worse. I also travelled to many countries including the U.S.A, Canada, Japan, Most of Europe, Sweden, and Denmark not once did I ever take out holiday insurance.

CLUMSY ME (Dyspraxia)

My clumsiness continued as I endeavoured to carry a tray full of breakfast meals to various residents in bed. I began to walk down a flight of stairs and tripped the tray went forward but I held it tight, the problem was all the contents shot off the tray and up the wall, down the stairs and all over me. I eventually landed at the bottom of the stairs, upside down in a very undignified manner. I called out to a cleaner nearby "Help!" But she had the Hoover on and was singing happily to herself, while the scrambled egg was dripping from my head. Fortunately, I suffered no injuries and continued to have accidents regularly. On one occasion we the care assistants were asked by our matron, to participate in some gardening, this was a big mistake. Especially asking me to mow the grass with petrol operated lawnmower, no sooner had I started it up, and it had a mind of its own. It began to move; I lost my balance and was being dragged along the ground. Eventually it stopped when it hit the path and spun onto its side, I was still holding it and found myself in a bush. When I arrived home, I was angry and embarrassed I told my mother the story "I'm a care assistant not a gardener" I said. Mother just laughed the more I said the more she laughed. She likened me to Frank Spencer a character played by Michael Crawford in a television comedy called 'Some mothers do hav em' I eventually saw the funny side of my dilemma and laughed too; I was unaware of dyspraxia that this time.

Even on holiday I wasn't safe, I was having a photograph taken in Germany beside the scenic river Rein. I was leaning against a pole posing when the pole began to rise taking me up with it. I discovered it was a level crossing and had to jump down fast. When I was in India a soldier asked me to accompany him to the airport luggage department, which was outside near the plane. On the way I slipped on the freshly polished stairs, and landed at the bottom of the stairs. On a flight to the U.S.A I managed to damage two seats. The first seat was due to a loose arm, I pulled it towards me and it came all the way off. The kind stewardess apologised for the faulty seat and placed me elsewhere, I was trying to get comfortable by adjusting the seat when I heard a crunch. The seat shot back rapidly causing my legs to fly up in the air and my head landed between a lady's legs.

Many other disasters took place, but I still insisted that I did not need holiday insurance. Infact the only time that I did take out insurance nothing happened. I realise now I will always be clumsy and feel sorry for my long-suffering wife, who picks up the pieces. I had been through twenty jobs before settling down as a care assistant at Nearfield house. My job at this place lasted thirteen years, I only left because I wanted to progress as there was no chance of promotion and I felt I needed to do something that would offer more prospects. I returned to shop work but couldn't settle and I became very depressed again dyslexia were holding me back. I was thirty and something triggered a reminder of my rape and I became suicidal, finally I told my mother and she was shocked, the night terrors got more intense and realistic as if I was reliving the entire ordeal over and over again. The doctor put me on antidepressants and I decided to work away for a while, I needed to start a new life and forget Lichfield. There were too many reminders of bad experiences and the reminder of my rape ordeal really hit home, especially as I blamed myself for getting in such a situation in London. Often the victim does this apparently, I ran away to find a new life, to escape from the world that I lived in, a cruel and callus place. Instead, I entered a real nightmare like I was being punished for running away.

I left home in Lichfield, for Blackpool and worked as a photographer this suited me well, I met my wife at this holiday centre and moved to Manchester. I returned to care work at a residential home and both Jayne and I started a family, we married a few years later and I began working at a nearby hospital, this gave me a real incentive to train as a nurse and so I went to college to gain qualifications in order to enter university. I had informed them that I could be dyslexic and received a little support. I obtained a certificate in welfare studies and an N.V.Q (National vocational qualification) in care this gave me the chance to apply for nursing I was accepted but did not inform them of my condition at first because I was embarrassed and felt I would be thrown off the course, I progressed until exam time then I had to confess. I was sent for tests at the universities educational support office and it was confirmed that I have dyslexia. I received a diploma in welfare studies at college while studying at university and graduated from the university of Salford with a diploma in nursing with support from the education centre. I began working as a staff nurse and now have four children who I observe for signs of dyslexia as I would not like them to experience the problems that I had, dyslexia remain a problem today however if you seek the right help life can be much more bearable, I don't blame my parents, little knowledge was available then, but today people can seek help and progress as far as they wish as long as they know who to approach for help and advice. Your life needn't be in a jar.......

LIFE IN A JAR

LIVING WITH DYSLEXIA

SIXTIES EDUCATION

The sixties were noted to be changing times with radical ideas, education witnessed changes with the rapid expansion of comprehensive schools and more freedom for teachers. The reforms took place under Harold Wilson's Labour government. According to Gary McCulloch (professor of education at London's institute of education) "What people often think of teachers in the 60s is that they had much more freedom". While pupils in the 60s still had to sit exams, there was no national curriculum and teachers had much more leeway.

The chief inspector of schools in England Mr David Bell stated that the teaching theories of the 60s and 70s were "plain crackers" He went on to say that "too much of the soft centred belief that children would learn if you left them to it". Mr Bell spoke of incoherent or non-existent curriculums, too many eccentric and unevaluated teaching methods, and too much of the totally soft centred belief that children would learn by themselves. He went on to praise the improvements of recent years.

Corporal punishment

The main form of discipline in the 60s and 70s was corporal punishment the incidence of caning or whacking varied from school to school. Some used a stick other a pump or a ruler and it was administered across the hand or bottom. Some teachers used their hand across the head of the pupil or a nice thick book.

In Chadsmead it was a selection of the ruler, cane or a smack round the head or legs, while Netherstowe comprehensive school was the slipper, pump, cane or hand. Corporal punishment was finally abolished in 1987 by parliament this was by a mere one vote. A retired truancy inspector spoke in favour of corporal punishment stating "When I was at school there was as often as not a disruptive pupil who distracted the rest of the class from their work. Once he had been caned the rest of us could get on with our studying. After you had felt the cane, you gained a healthy respect for it" which was bullshit.

In reality people with learning difficulties who may have lost their attention span had blackboard rubbers thrown at them, or children could be disruptive through shear frustration of not being able to understand. The problem with corporal punishment is it was misused and sometimes the wrong people got punished, this to my mind only stopped the disruption it did not solve the problem. It made me more fearful of teachers and less likely to perform, as it exasperated the problem (now known as dyslexia).

There has been attempt to reintroduce corporal punishment in state schools, doing so would be like going backward in time, when we need to strive forward and find other solutions to problems. Who wants to witness such cruelty again, certainly not me, asthmatic or other poor children suffering from stress? Some have even had panic attacks and worse, embarrassed by being exposed as thick or lazy, when all you want is an understanding teacher who knows how to teach dyslexic children.

My parent's point of view (Mrs Rita Sutton)

My mother explained how she felt about my past, regarding the subject of dyslexia.

'When my little boy started school, he was nervous. He found it difficult coping with his reading and writing, and as time went on, he was placed in a remedial class. This did not have a great deal of affect, with the teachers not understanding his problem; they had very little patience with him. Stephen was a quiet and sensitive child who kept most things to him. I also feel that my husband and myself were strict parents, perhaps this made us unapproachable at times. I would not begin to make excuses though I must say, living in the sixties was hard, and if you did not work there, was no income. Social security was means tested and when my husband needed support financially, we had to sell things to in order to eat. My other two children performed well at school, which puzzled us even more when Stephen failed to show signs of progress. The word 'dyslexia' was not known, and we had no idea that he needed a special method of teaching. Unfortunately, because of this Stephen's school life was not very happy and he became very frustrated. The sad part is all this could have been avoided, if he had been recognised as dyslexic/dyspraxic. Today however it is recognised, my son was diagnosed at forty, and has managed by his own merit to graduate from university with a diploma in nursing '. Another parent describes her son's condition from the point of view not just as a parent but a teacher. She is now a headmistress at a junior school where my own children attend as pupils. But years ago, she was faced a major problem. Her son was dyslexic.

My mother gave a very touching account of my school days, as does this next person who is a head mistress at my daughter's school.

Experience of a son with dyslexia

At an early age my husband and I realised that our son had a problem with his spelling all through primary school, teachers told us that he was a good reader and that the writing and spelling accuracy would come with time. Also, the fact that he was left-handed could be a problem.

By secondary school, his spelling remained a handicap, stopping him from getting good marks, even the science teacher marked him down, simply because he spelt oxygen wrong in a otherwise excellent science investigation. I as a teacher with English as my speciality, decided to do something about it. Every night, I went through spelling patterns with him, I bought a computer program for him and tried my best to help him. He was very upset and refused to do a lot saying "My mum, not my teacher "

Eventually having gained nine G. C. S. E s, his A' level teacher decided to test him for spelling dyslexia (known as Dysorthographia) This was particularly important as he would lose mark in exams, especially in geography. At the age of eighteen his spelling age was only eleven, but it was too late to do anything about it. He managed to gain four A 'levels and was accepted at Newcastle university to study for a B.Sc. in marketing. The university have been wonderful, at last after fifteen years he has had recognition. Clear testing and a clearer understanding as a dyslexic, he is allowed an additional forty-five minutes in exams. He is also predicted to have a 2.1 degree this summer and has an abundance of confidence, my husband and I are so proud of him ". For Mrs L. Johnson this was a story of success despite earlier educational problems. Many parents share these anxieties, concerning their child's education. Parents are even seeking answers on the Internet; the 'Dyslexic parents' group' is answering questions though not all cases involved have dyslexia. But problems in education still prevail and require addressing in order to avoid unnecessary heartbreak.

LIFE IN A JAR

LIVING WITH DYSLEXIA

WHAT BEING DYSLEXIC MEANS TO ME

My name is Kerry Bennett and to those of you" who do not know, I have recently started to work for the Dyslexic Institute as Communications Officer, based at Staines. However, there is some sort of irony behind my present position. I say this because I am dyslexic and I had my first assessment 10 years ago, at Staines.

I was 15 years old when my English teacher suggested to my parents that I be assessed.

Throughout my schooling my teachers had always wondered why I was above average in Science and Maths but yet poor at English and poorer still with Languages. I remember when the gentleman who conducted my assessment told me that he could confirm I was dyslexic, I could not help myself from bursting into tears in his office. I think it was the relief of finally knowing that there was a reason for my unusual spelling style and guess-the-correct-word reading. Although they were the only tears, I have ever shed over being dyslexic.

What does it mean to me, to be dyslexic? Well, what does it mean to be a non-impaired reader, to a non-impaired reading individual? I do not know the answer to the second question, so what is being dyslexic like? I mean this in the same sense as if you do not know hate, how can you experience kindness. I have never seen being dyslexic as a problem. I have always had a positive determined attitude towards my difficulties, perhaps even a little too complacent at times! However, I am not severely dyslexic and I appreciate how difficult it must be for those who are.

] do have my own coping strategies that I have developed with age which it would appear I have in common with other adult dyslexics who have written to me. I spell and read my memory and if I come across, I word I do not recognise I either guess what it is from the sentence or look it up in the dictionary and guess from the definition. However, I would be telling a little white lie if I said that I sailed through education and had no difficulties what so ever. My degree is in Human Biology and this involves learning a whole new scientific lingo.

For example, what does the word 'salpingopharyngeus' say and how should it be pronounced? I have no idea but I did learn to spell the word of-by-heart and that it is a muscle of the soft palate, found posterior to the tongue. I did find this aspect particularly difficult. I would spend hours learning to spell words like a parrot! because I just could not/cannot break the words down, in order to read what the letters in the word represent.

However, mine is not a sad story, as is the case for others. Despite being dyslexic, I am proud of what I have achieved and there is no use in wishing I were not dyslexic My name is Kerry and I am dyslexic. I am not 'Kerry the Dyslexic' and as such my achievements are separate from my difficulties!

By Kerry Bennett

My life as a dyslexic (A personal account from U.S.A)

I was born in a small rural town in Washington state in 1965. I am the youngest of 6 children, 11th maternal pregnancy in my mothers 36th year. Biological father is questionable. There is a history of prescription overuse and alcohol abuse in family and enutero. My introduction to alcohol was an unfortunate, unsupervised opportunity to drink hard alcohol to the point of intoxication at the age of three. Alcohol was sipped from parent's beverages at an early age. At the age of six, wine was a nightly dinner beverage in small quantities. All of this history, has been attributed by therapists to be a possible cause of my dyslexia.

I attended Kindergarten at the normal age of five. I struggled with staying quiet, being put in the back of the classroom as a punishment for my misbehaviour. I had limited attention span. During naptime, I was disobedient, unable to settle down and rest. I was given multiple punishments, all which became a challenge for me to increase the severity. My artwork was scrutinized for objects, such as purple turkeys with green legs, not being grounded.

In the first grade I attended a small school of less then 60 kids in K-12. I had individualized learning with the Dick and Jane series. Even then, more focused on the pictures then on the words and not holding comprehension to the written words. My family had evening reading, Charlie and the Chocolate Factory was the book at the time, and since I was too young to read, I would listen. I held great comprehension of the story through visualization. We moved prior to the end of my first-grade year at about age seven. Due to work situations, family reading fell wayside. There was a realization that some of my letters and numbers were backwards. I struggled with S and Z, B and D, G, A, and 3,5,7, 6, and 9. I actually had to memorize the direction and quiz myself before writing them, but often would still confuse the direction. The family moved again and I started the second grade all over again. I had a brilliant and insightful teacher who had me tested. I remember a few of us going to the hallway to be tested with numbers, letters, and comprehension, in addition to hearing. This was repeated at the end of the year and again in the third grade.

Throughout these years I did average, had a good attitude and played well with other children, but I learned the best at listening. At home, my father would read trivia to me, which I find easy to recall even today, from listening skills. I often would read from the opposite side of the breakfast table or from across the table from other siblings' schoolwork. I found reading from in an upside-down manner often faster and less straining on the eyes.

In the third grade I learned my first "trick" regarding my reading difficulties. The SRA reading cards were a competition in my environment. The smart kids would advance quickly to the silver level, while the children with reading problems would stay back in the green level. I would hide the card, pull the test, and look up the answer to each question, knowing that the reading was difficult and the comprehension was limited. I would score highly on the reading card and advance, therefore placing me at a higher level with the "smart kids". But when it came time to read aloud, I would become very embarrassed. Words and even entire lines would float off the page, to which my teacher would stop me, make mention of this mistake, and have me start over. Using

my finger to carefully follow along, I would try from the beginning through the giggles and comments from classmates.

It was in the fourth grade that I learned my newest "trick". We would be assigned a book report. Knowing that I could not read the book and already feeling the defeat, I would make up a book name, author, and story, and then write a book report on this book that doesn't even exist. I was soon discovered and punished. But the greater punishment seemed to be the idea of actually trying to read a book that I would simply give up on in the first few chapters. At this point, my fellow classmates were reading children's novels. I fell into a role of class clown to divert attention from my downfalls. I was put into music class and given the opportunity to play an instrument of choice. I first chose the bass, later changing to the guitar. In each scenario, I found the music impossible to comprehend. I not only struggled with memorizing which way letters and numbers were to be written, I now had to make a mental game of how to read musical notes. I would try, but continue to look at the page with a blank stare each time I would open the book. I did not have the comprehension, nor did I have a way to make sense out of the musical notes in order to memorize them and read them. I felt the dissection of reading and action at this point. I then tried the piano with a colour dot system. But this was a little easier to remember but again, there was no connection to the colour and a system that I could read and work with. I ultimately quit at music.

In the fifth grade, at age ten, I had the skills to learn quickly from listening and teach other classmates, but my reading was not developing. It was suggested to my parents to put me into a "special school for the gifted". My parents heard "retardation" again, I was taken out of that school to save the family from further embarrassment and put into a private Catholic school with small class sizes. My grades began to be noticed and excuses were made, such as, "it's a new school", "her parents are divorcing", "she needs glasses", but no one wanted to address the idea of dyslexia. At age 14 I was put into a high school where I was to take French. Here my inabilities to grasp the written language were magnified. I could not make the English language work fluently, and in syntax, many parts of the French language are reversed and my English then deteriorated as I tried to memorize rules and apply them to French or to English, confusing them together frequently. We were also given reading assignments from the bible, of which I would read, but I read the written word, while others could read the parable. I struggled to turn the word-by-word text in a loose context. My English class was the greatest struggle that year. We read Shakespeare. This was next to hopeless. On several occasions I tried with all of my might to read the pages, but I could not make sense of the words in their order, and my comprehension was less then three pages. My end result was to cheat and make massive amounts of crib notes to pass the final exam.

My tenth-grade year I was transferred again to a public school, and age fifteen, I was now shy and convinced I was just stupid and now had to make a new name for myself. My new role was a "tough kid" or a "troublemaker". This intimidated the teachers and fellow students so they would not challenge me to read aloud and rather then challenge my homework they would just fail me or give me a passing D. I failed geometry, twice, because I could not understand the subject matter and could not memorize the order of the theories. I did better in algebra. I did well in science because it was hands on and lots of pictures. I can remember studying from the captions under the pictures and spending exurbanite amounts of time talking with and learning from the

advanced science teacher, while watching the chemistry class with great envy knowing I could never have the ability to memorize and make sense of the chart. I again attempted French. This time I passed one semester with cheat notes and failed the next as the subject matter increased. I then tried Spanish, encouraged because it was easier. Now I mixed the syntax and words of English, French and Spanish all together and passed the first semester and failed the next with great frustration. I took business classes but my typing often had confused letters and so my wpm was low and although I could quickly correct my error, the actual wpm was barely passing and often I was the in the group of retested students. I tried to be a TA for the accounting teacher, marking tests by comparing them to the answer book, but would sometimes incorrectly mark the item on people's tests because I switched the numbers that I was looking at, causing concern about my abilities and feeling embarrassment. I was removed from this TA assignment. Skipping class became easier then attending and I soon jeopardized my ability to graduate. I took extra classes and passed with a 1.7 GPA.

My one golden moment was a senior year US History teacher by the name of Phil Waggoner who recognized my challenges and while others were taking their tests, he would quietly read the test to me and I would answer. When I would get stuck, or could not formulate the answer, we would look it up together to better understand the material. He understood dyslexia, and this was 1983. This was not embarrassing; this was a different opportunity to succeed. In conjunction with this semester, I was put into an English class that did basic sentence formations and your reading material was from magazine articles from which you would write a short essay. The reading assignment was short

so the comprehension was improved and this enabled me to practice my writing skills. We also wrote our own short stories which I had a skill for and a wonderful imagination.

I attended community college because my friends did. I struggled with basic classes and was placed in remedial English and math. My college courses struggled and I learned the tool of being in class, listening to lectures to succeed at a 50% level. I retook many classes and after nearly four years I completed a two-year education. Feeling like I just ran a marathon I took the next seven years off. I entered the work place where I quickly learned that you don't mention the word dyslexia; again, like in school and family life, you keep it a secret. I continued to self teach how to work in a business atmosphere and eventually returned to college for a second attempt. I repeated courses over and over again, but graduated with a Bachelor in a dual major program of Finance and Marketing.

At one stage in my mid-twenties, I considered doing formal testing in order to have additional time allowance on college testing. A management mentor took me into his office and behind closed doors advised, that if I ever took this test and it was known and on my employment record, I would most likely never work in finances or management. The perception of hiring personnel is that dyslexia is still considered stupidity (remember this was the early 1990's) and that it could severely hamper my opportunities in employment.

Not ever mentioning the handicap, I moved into a role of management with a major health insurance company and took on the role of financial analysis. I have moved on since that role, including owning my own business.

I have continued to work in a budgetary arena and do home repairs with some challenges but lessons learned.

I have learned in reflection that the ways that I cope are a.) With words, it is vital to proofread every document. Even emails must be reread for clarity and accuracy, b.) numbers are not learned in a string larger then about 3, but with some games with numbers I can remember the patterns. Numbers each have their own relationship; such as the number 34,719 would be literally remembered as three-four-seven-one-nine in a singsong manner. Anything else would leave opportunity for reversal; c.) I have learned that when doing home projects that require building skills, always assume I might be doing this in a backwards manner and look at it in reverse. Draw everything out, lay out your materials, and double check all measurements; d.) Most important, I have learned to ask questions. Be honest with folks and have them help you.

I now have entered a time in my life where a student at a school that I work at has approached me, and he was going to drop out of high school. He has the same challenges that I have faced over my life. I took the golden opportunity to share my life story with him briefly and encourage other avenues of learning and to embrace his uniqueness. He has since considered quitting once again, but has reversed his decision and is completing his high school education. He recognizes he can do anything he puts his mind to. It won't be easy and he may repeat classes some classes, but the opportunities that are now available to him are more then ever before. He is able to use books on tape for some of his reading assignments; he attends class regularly to catch the lectures and in my opinion is feeling far more comfortable with the challenges that lie ahead.

LIFE IN A JAR

LIVING WITH DYSLEXIA

FAMOUS DYSLEXICS

The famous singer and actress Cher, was in this predicament when her daughter Chastity was showing signs of being a poor student, Cher took her to their doctor to be tested, thinking that she had some sort of learning disability. Cher refused to believe that her daughter was stupid, she may have been a difficult personality, but not the rebellious type that Cher once was. Cher was surprised when the doctor announced his discovery, not only was Chastity dyslexic but also Cher. Thus, demonstrating that dyslexia is infact inherited, though more commonly passed down the male side of the family, which explains why I am observing my own sons for signs of dyslexia. Cher realised why she had so many problems at school, and why making long distance telephone calls was a problem, trying to dial numbers. Cher compensates for her dyslexia by having a sharp memory; she also made dyslexia one of her causes to fight for.

Without a doubt Cher demonstrates ability to act and sing well, giving fine performances in concerts and on film. One of her finest performances can be seen in a film called 'the mask '. Memorable hits with ex-husband Sonny Bono when they performed as a duet with hits like 'I got you babe 'to her solo career with hits like 'Gypsy's, tramps and thieves 'The sloopy song (is it in his kiss) 'and her biggest number one hit 'Believe 'Cher demonstrates that if your determined enough and willing to fight for what you believe in then you may well succeed, despite your disability. Many people have proven this point by showing similar courage and determination. Cher met Tom Cruise at a fund-raising convention in connection with dyslexia, Tom who is also known to have dyslexia compared notes with Cher and they became very close.

Closer to home actress Susan Hampshire pioneered the need for dyslexics in Britain, recognising a need from her past experience with this disability which was once called word blindness. Susan's dyslexia were undiagnosed until she was twenty-nine, again showing that dyslexia were very much a condition that went unnoticed as a disability. Susan like most dyslexics has her own way of coping with the condition. As an actress she has to learn her lines, she has a positive approach to learning her script by having two copies of her scripts. The first script she keeps at home and covers it with a special code. The second is for show, which she keeps in tact and takes it to rehearsals. The battered scribbled version is hardly out of her hand, she likes to give the impression that working on the script was effortless. But if a second copy cannot be obtained, the truth is revealed. Susan finds the best method of learning lines is by repetition, repeating the same words over and over again out loud, she states reading silently on a train means the text does not get absorbed. This is said to be due mainly to poor concentration one of the conditions we dyslexics are plagued with, probably why I used to get in trouble for daydreaming.

It is a known fact that in the acting business, an average script takes the average actor an hour and a half to two hours to learn. For a dyslexic like Susan, it would take three to five hours, and complete silence in order to concentrate. According to Susan dyslexic people have an aptitude for languages, spelling in languages such as French, Spanish and Italian is more straightforward, also dyslexics tend to be artistic and respond quickly to any visual test. Actor Kenneth More once remarked on Susan's dyslexia 'I have no recollection whatsoever of your having reading difficulties dyslexia? No? Infact people only became aware of her dyslexia when she did work for other dyslexics'.

Kenneth More had worked with Susan, on the long running television drama 'The Forsyte saga 'as part of an all-star cast. Once it was over Susan was offered many parts including a spot in the children's story program 'Jackanory' she immediately stated that she could not read from television prompts. Instead, she would learn the words from the entire book, this was said to be no problem for the B.B.C and the script had the perfect story for her. However, on the day she ended up reading the prompter to her dismay. They never asked her again.

Susan declares that she had good support from her mother when she educated Susan herself at her own school 'Had I have not been ' she said ' I would have been tormented like other dyslexics. Her mother was said to have formed a protective bond around her, in order to reduce her suffering, she helped her to learn. But even educated people like teachers need a greater understanding of the psychological and physiological conditions of dyslexia in order to help pupils

LIFE IN A JAR

LIVING WITH DYSLEXIA

BILL'S STORY

In an article published by the Sunday times magazine, entitled forced to fail with a subheading just as direct saying He's not stupid, he's DYSLEXIC the author discusses some of the problems encountered in school today. Oxford's professor John Stein spent twenty years of his life studying dyslexia, he explains about the visual problems that a dyslexic encounter such as words vibrating or jumping about, he suggests that this may be due to the magnocells that see movement which make the eyes wobble minutely. Large print can help, or guided reading with a straight edge. I personally found a ruler or the edge of a hardback book cover useful. Also, the use of colour cellophane, or a patch over one eye, to steady the wobble.

My experience with plastic overlay was inspired by Bill Thomson on 21st March 2000 (read Bill's story in this chapter) It certainly works for me, also tinted glasses seem to help to some degree, though not nearly as affective as yellow plastic .at this been known at school perhaps I would have improved and felt more confident. But how much help is at hand in schools today? Sadly, so many teachers still fail to recognise dyslexia, they see only the obvious signs such as reading, writing, and sometimes spelling. They often miss the behavioural aspects, the fatigue, and clumsiness and short-term memory problems. The LEA s rough diagnostic is said to be in appropriate, the child can only be deemed dyslexic if his reading ability falls into the bottom 1% for his age, but reading is no test of dyslexia. I could read reasonably well by the age of twelve, however my spelling was atrocious. I could have scored 1% for reading, but zero for spelling. Because of this fact alone dyslexics can be missed and receive no special help. A lot of dyslexics still fall into remedial groups such as I did, this is where the schools' special needs budget tends to go.

But remedial teachers have proven to be of no use to dyslexics, the brighter dyslexic misses out even more because they are disqualified for special help, and so they struggle on encountering problems with sound, spelling and short-term memory. This is when the hard battle to survive in the education system begins to become unendurable and rebellion begins. One person who recognise this is Elizabeth Henderson head of old-field primary school in Maidenhead; she has been instrumental in introducing multi-sensory teaching at the school. As a dyslexic herself she empathises with her pupils, said to be hopeless at school she was eventually chucked out for disruptive behaviour. Henderson uses the Aston test, which takes approximately an hour; this is conducted on a one-to-one basis with a child generating graphs with peaks and troughs indicating strengths and weaknesses. The child is tested from entry to school and monitored, parents are encouraged to get involved in their child's education plan. The more severe cases receive special help this is what old field considers good standard teaching practice.

I would certainly agree with them, and wish this system had existed in my days at school. Another problem dyslexics have is careful sequencing, learning left from right and days of the week. I tend to rely on precise detailed instruction that involves someone explaining what they want or on a shopping list giving details of required items instead of a brief outline, which can often be misinterpreted for a number of similar products. Short-term memory problems can cause so many mistakes; this is why I tend to carry a pad and pen around in my pocket, in case I need to take phone messages or record details about a situation.

LIFE IN A JAR

LIVING WITH DYSLEXIA

RICHARD HOWARTH'S STORY

It was with some trepidation that I entered Chadsmead junior school at the age of ten (or there about). Having just arrived from Gods own county of Yorkshire, here stood alone a small skinny young boy with a strong accent in a strange and formidable environment. I knew no one at all. However, I was going to meet my best and lifelong friend in this place little did I know.

I was placed in the first instance in the B stream with Mrs Abbott. She had as I recall a strong accent of the Brummy nature. This proved to be a problem to both of us. Alas I didn't fit in very well with this group, mainly because I could not, however hard I tried, learn my times tables. So therefore, I was relived of my rank (milk monitor) and banished into the baron and icy wastes of a hut at bottom of the school the remedial class. Here things changed and how.

A very kindly lady called Mrs Coleman met me. She sat me next to chap called Steven. He was asked to help through the interim of my new class. Little did I know he would become my best and life long friend. We became brothers very soon, and it now, almost forty years later becomes apparent why. We could not, properly understand the written word. (I know this is a long-winded way of describing dyslexia but I don't know how to spell it) One glorious moment at this school was the school nativity was, with the obligatory tea towel on my head, I shone like the star of Bethlehem. Since that moment I realized I could work an audience. This became very useful in later life.

Onward to the brand new Netherstowe comprehensive. With our new uniforms and side by side Steven Robert Sutton and myself walk into the BIG school. Same form and mostly the same the same classes, thank God, we settled into secondary education. This of course proved a little difficult because we could no not read, and know one really understood that. Thanks be to God, we had each other to lean on at that time. Notwithstanding, I had a good time at Netherstowe and I was very sad to leave that place. I would miss Mr Knowles, Mr. Bower and the rest whose names I can't remember. Oh yes, the lovely Miss Ash and the red head that taught English.

We moved to the Godforsaken land of our fathers Wales. A terrible place. I missed Lichfield. My mate Steve had to come and stay to help me with this awe full place. Of that I am eternally grateful. There was great excitement when Steve arrived. This was only matched when he came to visit some thirty odd years later in Yorkshire.

I was sent to a local secondary school whose name I cannot even begin to spell, and what a shock that was. A total lack of discipline. No uniform, leaking roofs. It was then I realized how lucky we were at Netherstowe, as Mr Bower had told us many times. He was a very wise man.

A teacher in this welsh school who was about to retire saw there was something about me and although I was unaware at the time he spoke to my parents and suggested I should re-take my 11+ and try for the grammar school. This was the first time I heard the word dyslexia.

Well, this I did, and entered Lewis's boys' grammar school shortly afterwards. This time a tall skinny boy with a strong accent entering a new and daunting place.

LIFE IN A JAR

LIVING WITH DYSLEXIA

BETTER SCHOOLS AND A BRIGHTER FUTURE

Cliff Warwick who is now Swansea city and Swansea counties chief SEN adviser was appointed In March 1996 due to a need to reorganise the local government. He was chosen because of his reputation of being a special needs champion, he wanted to pull all the rightful monies into the areas were it could be most effective namely dyslexic friendly mainstream schools for the mildly and moderately affected and a in house high level provision for the more severely affected pupils. After discussions with parents, who offered their suggestions progress was made.

A year later Warwick sent two of his SEN advisers for dyslexic institute training and both the B.D.A and parents were pleased with the progress. It is noted that today all secondary schools in Swansea have a B.D.A accredited teacher, and 50% of primary school and rising. Time is taken to consider financial priorities and organise the budget more effectively, maybe some day other counties will follow their lead. Another problem area generally is the methods used to assess the special needs of dyslexics in other areas, For instance it is dependant on local experts such as psychologists, language experts and occupation therapists among others agreeing the criteria and defining the severity of the dyslexia. So many problems occur due to this method, when will people learn that they could have gifted people amongst them, they could easily be suppressing an incredible talented person.

SCHOOL'S TODAY

Other schools seem to be recognising the need for more input including my son's school (Rosehill Methodist community school) where I help in class, and Chadsmead primary school where I went in the 60s. The schools teach using Jolly phonics and also make use of a multiphobic system with children with special needs. This demonstrates that progress has finally taken place at schools and gives hope for dyslexic children across the nation.

JOLLY PHONICS

In my son Michael and Daniels school (Rosehill Methodist community school) they use a system called 'Jolly phonics', this system is introduced in reception class and develops with the children through school. But how does it work and is it effective?

Jolly phonics is a foundation for reading and writing; it is designed to introduce letters and sounds in an enjoyable way. This guide is said to provide background advice for parents and teachers, the literature provided with jolly phonics explains the principles behind jolly phonics so that the understanding of teaching and ability of helping a child is much better.

Parent support is important as children rely on praise and encouragement. All children work at their own pace, but dyslexic children tend to need extra praise and encouragement. In some cases, extra aids are required to read such as coloured overlays to read with as in scotopic sensitivity syndrome. Sometimes concentration is lost and at this time teaching should stop for a while so that the child should not endure undue pressure.

With jolly phonics there are five basic skills these are: -

Learning the letter sounds
Learning letter formation
Blending
Identifying sounds in words
Spelling the tricky words

LETTER SOUNDS

In jolly phonics the 42 main sounds of English are taught and not just the alphabet (which I used to learn parrot fashion) the sounds are in seven groups. Some sounds are written in two letters such as ee and or these are called digraphs. Each sound has an action, which helps children remember the letters; it also makes learning much more fun. Children tend to progress as letters are pointed out to them, they do the actions and sound it. This is a joy to watch as they obviously enjoy it, I wish we had been taught in such a manner.

The letters are introduced not in alphabetical order as I remember being taught, but in groups the first being s,a,t,i,p,n this is because they make more simple three letter words than any other six letter words, interesting enough b and d are introduced in different groups to avoid confusion.

Some sounds have more than one way of being written (this is the dyslexics nightmare) these are initially taught in one form, then the alternate spelling are introduced later. This is said to take unnecessary pressure off children.

THE FORMATION OF LETTERS

The formation of letters is introduced once the child is taught to hold a pencil correctly, the child is then taught to write each letter beginning with easier letter formations and progress from there. They practice writing the same letter over and over again at school and at home following dotted shapes.

BENDING

Bending is a process of saying the individual sounds in a word then running them together to make a word. Sounding out words like C-A-T and making CAT or C-A-R to make CAR. This is a way all children tend to learn and improve with practice. Digraphs are represented by two letters such as SH, children learn to sound these digraphs as SH. Some words cannot be blended such as WAS, SAID and ONE. Unfortunately, many of these are common words, the irregular parts have been remembered. These are called tricky words or a nightmare to a dyslexic like myself.

MULTISENSORY PHONICS

The structured multisensory approach looks the most attractive for me, I could relate to this method. Infact it is noted that dyslexic adults who have tried to learn by conventional teaching methods need extra input that allows for a more versatile approach. The multisensory learning approach allows for an unlocking of the written word as never before thought possible. At last, a way to help dyslexic people and provide the learner with a way through, understanding the true meaning of words rather than just seeing them on a piece of paper.

The multisensory approach allows the learner to use all their senses, to hear the letters sounded to touch the letters and feel the shapes of plastic letters and to put pictures with letters or words. I tend to remember more from pictures when I construct cupboards from kits rather than read instructions, and more often than not I can assemble it without any problems (providing all the pieces are in the box).

My wife Jayne sent me to the shop for a children's analgesia (pain killer) she showed me the packet and I brought back the correct item. Had she just asked me I may have bought the wrong item.

TEACHING DYSLEXICS

It is important to remember that in order to teach dyslexics you need to know a little about their needs. The teaching methods with dyslexics tend to place great emphasis on phonics "In this they are directed at the what is for many dyslexics the greatest area of difficulty" Ellis (1993)

Owing to the short-term memory and attentional problems dyslexics require a form of 'over learning' (Thomson 1990)

Please note, "there are many children who are unable to respond to rote phonological or multi-sensory approach despite skilled teaching" (Lewis, 1996).

Ellis (1993) points out "several studies have shown that dyslexics can make reasonable progress when given systematic instruction, but the dyslexics in these studies are usually engaged in all sorts of reading related activities".

Learning to read may not require the memorisation of phonic rules or lists of words. Such sub skills could be acquired during the course of reading, (Pumfrey and Reason, 1991)

Individual assessments are carried out with the understanding that "The uniqueness of each child's pattern of abilities, attainments and difficulties is well accepted" (Pumfrey and Reason, 1991). This would most certainly be the logical approach for dyslexic pupils, the only danger is that an individual assessment may lead to treating the symptoms rather than the problem.

Tomson (1990) suggests that "although one could teach to a weakness (the auditory or phonetic deficits of a dyslexic) one should also circumvent the major problem by presenting the written language in alternative forms, namely visual and kinaesthetic". Through oral spelling, read covered up said again.

If someone could see through my eyes, or perhaps connect probes from my brain to theirs then they would understand my dilemma. My multiple difficulties are only apparent when certain situations arise such as reading, writing, using public transport, taking phone messages and other activities in life. What is normal to me is abnormal to you; I don't have a problem with that does you?

I will say thank God for inventions such as word processors, computers and any other invention that helps me to do certain tasks.

PHYSICAL PROBLEMS OF DYSLEXIA KNOWN AS DYSPRAXIA

Physical inadequacies in the form of clumsiness (like not being able to tie shoe laces) is a notable problem but sometimes not seen as a problem associated with dyslexia, but as Critchley (1970) points out there is a notable problem there.

Helen Irlen identifies the perceptual abnormalities of that cause visual dyslexia.

Scotopic sensitivity syndrome, which causes visual distortions that, is highlighted as: -

Light sensitivity: people can usually accommodate the high contrast and glare

Visual resolution: Usually people can see print without distortion

Span of focus: people can usually perceive groups of words

Sustained focus: people are able to sustain focus even in a relaxed state.

Note that visual dyslexic people have none of these abilities and have to take steps to reduced lighting; plastic overlays and tinted glasses help reduce this problem.

Teachers and tutors alike should be aware of students or pupils struggling at school, college or university and make the effort to learn about some of the difficulties involved. I have merely highlighted the problems involved and provide some help and support to students with learning difficulties.

BRIGHTSTAR

A new concept has emerged, Brightstar is said to be a unique technology based on a new scientific visual stimulus that is tailored to your body to aid communication areas of the brain. It stimulates eye tracking said to make it easier to scan and recognise words. Stimulates visual neural pathways helping the brain to process information faster and more affectively. Stimulates the cerebellum improves the timing necessary to execute reading and writing.

Brightstar boasts that it can help in just six weeks using revolutionary technology and tuition that is tailored to your unique needs. Before beginning the programme, Brightstar's teachers will identify particular difficulties you and your child may have with reading, recognising words and spelling as well as writing, memories and processing information. The Internet article also states that the initial assessment establishes whether you have the symptoms of dyslexia and gives them an accurate way to measure how much Brightstar helps.

They offer press reports that support their work and celebrities such as Duncan Goodhew (who is dyslexic) seems to recommend it. Personally, I have never tried this method and cannot comment.

Press reviews of Brightstar

"If you or your child is dyslexic, then you probably aware of the feelings of frustration and isolation that can appear as a direct result of dyslexia". Editorial that emphasises the problem that dyslexia have on people.

Swimming star Duncan Goodhew tells Suzanne Savill explains why he devotes so much time to promote the cause of peoples suffering from dyslexia and the benefits of this treatment.

Chris Pragnell was helped by Brightstar after doctors discovered that he had dyslexia South London press explains how this occurred on the Brightstar web site. Visit this web site and read more.

The more I study about dyslexia, the better I understand myself and some of the problems that I face on a daily basis. It also puts the past in perspective, those days of struggling to understand why I did certain things in various situations. The strategies I used over the years worked to help me develop and survive school days and beyond. But these strategies meant doing things the long way around and I have had to learn to take short cuts in order to achieve tasks more quickly and meet time constraints. Herald (Glasgow, Scotland), p 10 18-Nov-2004 By Raymond Duncan;

Sir Jackie Stewart makes plea for special needs teachers

SIR Jackie Stewart yesterday called for every Scottish primary school to have a special needs teacher to help identify children with dyslexia at an early age.

The plea from the former Formula 1 world champion, who is dyslexic, came at the launch of a merger of two charities working on the learning disability, which affects more than 10% of the Scottish population.

The Scottish Dyslexia Trust and Dyslexia in Scotland have pooled their resources to form the Stirling-based Dyslexia Scotland, backed by a (pounds) 50,000 donation from Sir Jackie, president of the new organisation. At the launch in the Scottish Parliament yesterday, Sir Jackie said he had grown up believing himself to be ''dumb, thick, and stupid All three I qualified for in a major way. Had it not been for sport, I don't know how it might have turned out.

''It might have been crime, drugs, or alcohol. It surely would have been unhappiness and probably non-achieving.''So, therefore, the risk to all those dyslexia sufferers in this country is very serious if we cannot give them help.''

Sir Jackie, who was accompanied at the press conference by Jack McConnell, first minister, and Sir Peter Burt, a former head of the Bank of Scotland and now chairman of ITV, said the key was early screening and early diagnosis. He said that dyslexia affected a great many people of all ages, including an immense body of adults who were so shy and insecure that they were frightened to admit they could not spell or read correctly.

The racing legend said that 10% of the population suffered from dyslexia or similar ailments. ''That's a fantastic potential being lost and not being looked after. It is a shocking loss for young people not to reach their true potential just because they can't read or write. 'We can put Scotland on the map, I believe, by creating early detection of learning disabilities and ideally, we should get in the position of having a special needs teacher in every single primary school in this country. We can lead the world in that."

Sir Peter, two of whose three sons are dyslexic and who will chair the merged organisation, said: "I'm enthusiastic about the opportunity we have to make a real difference to people's lives. And, as you'd expect from an ex-banker, I'm extremely enthusiastic about the enormously attractive cost-benefit figures that come out from making sure that people with dyslexia can achieve their potential.

"I'm sure that, with the enthusiasm and expertise of the volunteers and staff, combined with the resources and support of the Scottish Executive, we're going to be able to provide a new dawn for people with learning difficulties in Scotland."

Sir Peter said that too many people with dyslexia wound up "condemned to a less than healthy life". He added: "A large number end up in prison. Given the cost of keeping people in prison, reducing the chance of someone being sent to prison because he or she is trapped in a spider's web of frustration makes strong economic sense."

Mr McConnell, who promised £100,000 funding over the next two years for the charity to work with schools to develop best practice on supporting dyslexic children, said the launch was extremely significant.

He added: "It says loud and clear that young people with dyslexia in Scotland should have no limits put on their ambition. "We have a duty to ensure future generations have more support and understanding, and therefore a better start in life."

BrightStar's mission is to help people with dyslexia achieve life changing goals. BrightStar requires only 6 weeks to enhance your life.

BrightStar takes less than 90 minutes a week of your time. The programme involves:

- An Initial Assessment
- Two 20-minute Brightstar sessions
- One 40-minute one-on-one tutoring session
- A Final Assessment

The programme times are scheduled to when suits you, so you can visit us early in the morning, during lunch breaks, in the evening after work, or during weekends. It is incredible to think that such a short time commitment can provide such benefits – but as over 1500 people have found out, 6 weeks is all you need.

DDAT (Dyslexic, Dyspraxia and Attention disorder Treatment)

Who We Are?

DDAT (also known as DORE Achievement Centres) help children and adults affected by learning difficulties achieve their full potential. Whether you've been formally diagnosed or you are living with symptoms associated with dyslexia, dyspraxia or ADHD, the DDAT programme might be beneficial. Over the past 3 years, our exercise-based programme has helped more than 16,000 children and adults.

Our Approach

The DDAT individualised exercise programme is aimed at minimising or eliminating Cerebellar Developmental Delay (CDD), the likely cause of many learning difficulties. The programme directly addresses the physiological source of the problem by using exercises that stimulate the cerebellum and allow you to process information more rapidly. Our approach is non-invasive and drug free.

What is the cerebellum?

The cerebellum is a relatively small part of the brain, but the effects it can have on the body, emotions, and memory are enormous. Half the cells in the brain are concentrated in the cerebellum and it has a vast number of connections to the cerebrum, or "thinking brain." Exciting new research has shown that the cerebellum is responsible for integrating sensory information to allow efficient learning to take place.

What is cerebellar developmental delay (CDD)?

The thinking brain, the part of the brain responsible for intelligence, is usually quite healthy in our clients. In fact, many of those who suffer from learning difficulty symptoms are above average intelligence. But if the neural pathways - the connectors that link the thinking brain and the cerebellum - aren't yet fully developed, the cerebellum can't process information quickly enough. We call this cerebellar developmental delay, or CDD. One in 6 people have symptoms of CDD, yet most go undiagnosed.

How do I know if I have CDD?

If you've been diagnosed as suffering from dyslexia, dyspraxia, ADD or ADHD, or you recognize yourself in the list of symptoms, you may well have CDD. We are able to detect CDD through the various tests we run with new clients.

What is automaticity and is it related to learning processes?

Research has shown the cerebellum is highly active during learning processes and becomes much less so once a skill becomes automatic. Throughout the day we perform many skilled actions without having to think about each individual step separately in order to complete the task. For instance, take the task of driving a stick shift car. When learning how to perform this task an individual will think about the sequence of events and then what needs to be completed within each step-in order to complete the task successfully. Through practice and repetition the individual will then be able to perform this task almost without thinking, i.e. it becomes automatic. For persons with learning difficulties, automaticity is not achieved for many skills. Simple skills such as reading, writing, and spelling remain very difficult. The DORE exercises, using repetitive coordination and balancing activities, help develop the capacity for automaticity.

Can the cerebellum be improved, or changed?

Yes, the capability of the brain for physiological change is medical principle known as "neuroplasticity." With the DORE exercise program, we can stimulate the cerebellum to create new neural pathways which speed up the processing of information, and in doing so, help with learning, language, emotion and motor skills. Once your cerebellum has been developed, our research suggests it stays that way.

The Results

Balsall Common School Research Results

Independent tests on school children on the programme showed staggering results

- **Progress in reading was more than 3 times greater than in the previous year**
- **Progress in comprehension was nearly 5 times greater than in the previous year**
- **Progress in writing was 17 times greater than in the previous year**

After 12 months of DDAT exercises, many children reported huge improvements in areas such as

- **Self esteem**
- **Sporting ability**
- **Concentration**

After 12 months of completing the DDAT programme 76% of pupils reported progress...

LIFE IN A JAR

LIVING WITH DYSLEXIA

ASTHMA AND DYSLEXIA

My elder brother Jim tried to get me to defend myself as I was being bullied at school, he wanted me to be tougher, but due to my asthma and being under weight I was weak, besides a gang used to protect me at school. My brother did prevent me from harm and taught me to be strong, I was able to defend myself from armed attackers in places like Coventry and later abroad in New York and California. So, I am grateful to my brother, he did help me a lot in the past.

My father felt sorry for me, but tried not to show it in case I became worse. My mother did show her concern but was over protective and it did make my attacks worse but this was only because she loved me and wanted to help me as a sickly child, not being able to breath was frightening and if someone panics around you then you panic more. I admire both my brothers for their strength and determination.

So, what was the answer, a new school, new environment that knows? After eight years of asthma, I faced the worst attack ever, and I thought I was dying. It was on holiday at Mablethorpe near Skegness, on the east coast of England. The year was 1967, it was a hot summer in the middle of August, and the Beatles were in the charts with a song called 'All you need is love'. The east coast is flat, and when the wind blows it really knocks you out, especially asthmatics like me takes your breath away, literally.

ASTHMA -CAUSE AND EFFECT

Asthma can be a dreadful and a lethal illness that renders its victim completely helpless and fearful of their destiny. Asthma by definition is described as a common and chronic inflammatory condition of the airways; the cause is not completely understood. As a result of inflammation is hyper responsive and they narrow easily in response to a wide range of stimuli. This causes restricted airflow in the lungs, and difficulty for the patient to exhale harmful gases. Evidence shows that asthma is on the increase in both Britain, and the United States. Though the death rate is not so severe.

My own experience of asthma began when I was diagnosed at four years old. My condition was said to be caused by traumatic experiences such as, starting school, the doctor called it nervous asthma, this comes as no surprise to me now, as I reflect back to my early childhood, however at the time it was very frightening not knowing why I had trouble breathing, especially at the age of seven when I was on the verge of bronchial pneumonia. I remember leaving my grandparents house at the age of four, they were my fathers' parents, who I loved dearly especially my grandmother, we shared the same birthday, she too had asthma so we could relate to each other having a common problem. I remember the removal van arriving and looking through the bay window in the living room. We were leaving Birmingham for a place called Lichfield in Staffordshire, still in the Midlands but eighteen miles from my grandparents.

Our new home was on the second floor of a three-story flat which was in an L shape, we were in the mid corner section. It seemed very communal, quite a friendly community, most of the neighbours were nice and kept their gardens neat and tidy. Some of us were classed as the Birmingham over spill, (people from Birmingham who required housing) and it also meant the children would require schooling in the area. My initial experience with school was certainly not a happy one, as I previously stated in the chapter about having dyslexia, the teachers used to shout at me, especially my own teacher who was said to be suffering from some nerve problem. She used to accuse me of being insolent (what she called dumb insolence) just because I was quiet, we used to get sent to the headmistress and slapped on the legs or bottom.

This kind of punishment was administered regularly in the nineteen sixties, all part of school discipline as was caning, use of the ruler across the hands, and in some cases a slap around the head. Infect it was so bad children were afraid to ask to leave the classroom in case they were chastised. I wanted the toilet at one point and had a severe attack of diarrhoea, to my embarrassment I was so afraid of asking I had an accident messing my trousers and bear legs, it was awful my elder brother had to escort me home, as we walked home, he kept his distance, owing to my condition. It must have looked so obvious to others what I had done. When I arrived home my mother was very angry seeing me in such a state, she said looking back at the incident, but it wasn't my sons fault it was the teacher who was so strict and wouldn't allow him to go out to the toilet, or maybe he was afraid to ask.

My asthma appeared about this time, coughing and wheezing gasping for breath, with little relief but to just inhale vicks vapour rub, which was administered by placing the vicks substance in a bowl of boiling water, placing a towel over my head, and inhaling the fumes. Although I felt relief it was a very unpleasant experience and one, I will remember for the rest of my life, infact when I care for someone with respiratory problems, it reminds me of my experiences of asthma. Another way of relief I discovered was to push my abdomen against a windowsill, and push the air out. Today of course there are many ways of getting relief from an asthma attack, help is plentiful people need not suffer unnecessarily, also schools have changed dramatically, however the issue of school bullying continues which is discussed later in the book.

I lost a lot of school due to asthma; this was no loss for me as I used the time wisely by studying ways to learn to read and write, unaware of my dyslexia or the meaning of my disability. In extreme attacks of asthma, I used to panic; I could also sense my parent's anxieties which unknown to them made me worse. I remember pressing my stomach against the window sill, this seemed to make me more comfortable, today the experts would suggest that the patient use a table and a pillow for comfort, this is for purposes of posture and positioning of the lungs.

At the age of twelve came my worst and last attack of asthma in eight years, we were on holiday as a family at Mablethorpe near Skegness on the east coast of England. It was very flat country with strong sea breezes that seemed to take my breath away. I was well for a few days, and then it happened, wheezing, unable to breath, curled up in discomfort. I was taken to the holiday camp doctor who prescribed suppositories, they looked like bullets of cream cheese my father used to have to administer them into my rectum, they began to feel very uncomfortable it was like a burning sensation that made me feel sick, but they worked. We were there for two weeks, we returned home on the train, to my parent's astonishment as soon as we arrived in the Midlands, my symptoms improved until I was fully recovered. I was taken to the doctors by my mother however the doctor wanted to see me alone, He explained the meaning of stress induced asthma and said it was a condition of the mind, that I could control it was up to me, after which he called my mother back in and stated "He will never get asthma again "this proved to be the case, as I have only ever suffered from allergic reactions to dust and certain animals such as cats. My life is free from asthma as long as I am sensible and keep away from the trigger factors such as dust, hay and cats and of course smoking, which was once a habit of mine.

Today their are a team of specialists who are devoted to helping asthma sufferers, these people are asthma nurses who work in hospitals, clinics and in the communities ensuring patients receive the right care, are educated in their condition and know how to administer their medication correctly, also they can offer support to the carers, parents or guardians by explaining to them that they should not be alarmed, stay calm for the patients sake and help their child or relative by making them as comfortable as possible, keeping them calm and medicated . Life need not be in a jar for the asthmatic as long as they receive the right support and take their medication sensibly. Having said this it is disturbing to find that asthma is on the increase and the reasons are not fully known, one theory is the ever-increasing problem of pollution.

My parents were understandably anxious about me, my father really felt concerned about my condition. He was inclined to hide his true feelings, but my mother knew him well, and could read between the lines. Mother was more open and revealed her feelings, she explained how she felt looking back on those days ' I remember those days well, my son suffering helplessly wheezing and being unable to breath properly. Not having known anyone with asthma, it was very worrying when my son had an attack, we would try and stay calm, but the more he struggled the more anxious we became and he could sense our anxiety. This made him worse until we had hit a vicious circle, like a merry go round unable to get off. When he had bronchial asthma and was on the verge of pneumonia, I was really frightened and unable to cope with the situation. He told his younger brother he was going to die, I panicked but tried not to show it but felt so helpless. This was thirty-seven years ago before the use of nebulising drugs or inhalers, all we had was vicks vapour rub that could be melted in a bowl of hot water and inhaled under a towel. I always blame myself for being so ignorant and unable to reassure my little boy" But she was not to blame if information wasn't freely available at this time, beside as Dr Brown my GP said it was caused by stress, remove the stress and it will go.

Looking back my parents should not be blamed for not knowing about asthma or dyslexia, as so little was known in those days. Today we are blessed with an abundance of knowledge, readily available on request and medications. We also receive so much support from the professional bodies in the medical and educational profession; help lines are also available offering full support. Parents need not feel anxious about their children, if they remain calm the condition can be stabilised by medication or a trip to the hospital if you are unduly concerned. Very few asthmatics become chronically ill and even less die due to their condition from the day of diagnosis the patient should be educated in the management of their own asthma, children adapt remarkably well to changes in their lifestyle. We need to adapt with them for their own benefit and happiness. Schools should be more pupil friendly and offering support for those suffering from stress or anxiety, showing concern for those suffering as I know many do. I wish it had been the case when I was at school. My granddaughter has panic attacks which seem to stem from anxiety with her dyslexia, she has a place to go away from her class in school. One day a male school friend was helping her with her reading and the teacher shouted at the boy for talking, this showed her up and she had a panic attack. I was once shown up in class at senior school when a remedial teacher took me out of class for a remedial lesson, how embarrassing the whole class knew.

Preventing asthmatic attacks

As previously stated asthmatics tend to over react to allergies, which trigger off narrowing of the airways in some bronchial hyperactive (B .H. R). For this reason, it is advisable to avoid these triggers wherever necessary, asthmatic may get symptoms from the following trigger factors: -

House dust mites, pollens, Animals, Exercise, Cold or warm air, Deep inhalation such as fits of laughter, Drugs such as anti inflammatries, Foods including additives, Pregnancy and menstruation, Emotion i.e stressful situations, Smoke, Dust even talcum powder, Sprays and perfume.

Swimming is said to be good for asthma because it encourages good steady breathing posture is also important sitting or standing in an upright position.

Allowing the lungs to expand properly. Avoiding stressful situations whenever possible, remaining calm and relaxed. Being aware of the early signs wheezing, tightening of the chest, shortness of breath or dypsnoea, or perhaps just a cough to begin with. Try to avoid people who show signs of beginning with a cold, or suffering from influenza, as this can be more harmful to you.

Take your medication as prescribed, and not when you become very ill. Remember prevention is better than cure; I should know I've been there.

Having discussed asthma as a condition, and explain the symptoms, and how to prevent an attack, let's look at an unexpected possible cause namely dyslexia! You are probably as surprised as I was to find that there is said to be a connection between asthma, allergies, eczema and dyslexia. What an unpleasant thought, but this explains my childhood problems and puts everything into perspective, infact this was the final part of my jigsaw, this made the picture complete all the answers to my problem's could be summed up in one word 'dyslexia'. The information came from a study by Professor John Stein head of Oxford's department of physiology who spent no less than twenty years investigating dyslexic brain function.

According to Stein early man needed a highly developed, right brain visuo -spatial awareness to know where he was, in order to keep him on the right line figuratively speaking. Stein explained that the development of language and a long time after reading and writing is about the most difficult thing the brain has to master. Thus, are species becoming left brain dominant, which today is larger than the right. He also noted than the chromosome sites implicated in dyslexia are very to the genes that control the auto immunity system and therefore dyslexics are especially prone to allergies, asthma and eczema. Stein suggests that key cells in dyslexics were once attacked and injured by the body's own defence system during foetal development. This could explain a lot about my condition, I had eczema as a baby, asthma from the age of four and allergies to a number of things from pollen, to fur, food and drink products and a wide range of item's.

Stein concludes by adding that dyslexia may be nature's way of keeping our mental specialities in the proper balance or literally on the right track. His final words were "Dyslexia would not be so common if it's effects were wholly detrimental ".

I have been relatively free from asthma from the age of twelve, and only recently has it reoccurred which I viewed as stress related, as I did as a child. However, it is less severe, and controlled on inhalers (salbutamol) when required which is not often. The allergies affect me on a regular basis, but I try to avoid the allergens or trigger factors. I still consider myself more fortunate than some people, who get through life in pain and anguish on a daily basis. Yet these people show so much courage as do those who live in perpetual fear from being physically or mentally abused.

Fortunately, I hardly suffer today, but if I did or if it reoccurred like it can in later life then I can be prepared. This is why I want to help other sufferers of what my doctor once described as a beastly disease called asthma. I would not want anyone to suffer like I did, whether it is from asthma or any of my other problems discussed in this book. Rather I would be inclined to help by providing information relevant to their needs, or give details such as addresses of someone who is more skilled in the given subject that they might make contact and discuss their situation or needs. I hope this book achieves its objectives and helps many people along the way. Good health to you! .

LIFE IN A JAR

LIVING WITH DYSLEXIA

PRISON AND DYSLEXIA

A report written by The British dyslexia Association and Bradford Youth Offending Team entitled 'Unrecognised dyslexia and the route to offending'.

There is evidence of a "route of offending" among young people which apparently started with difficulties in the classroom, who continue with low self esteem, poor behaviour and school exclusion which then end with offending. It is said that children and young people with dyslexia are more likely to take this route, because of the difficulties they face with learning. In recent years a number of studies have revealed as high as 10% of the population and the figures are staggering as reports come in across Britain.

A project set up to deal with this problem aims to improve the way in which the dyslexic young people who come into contact with the criminal justice system are supported and managed to reduce re-offending.

The objectives to do this are to map all elements of the youth criminal justice system, observe current working practices of the system, observe and evaluate the extent to which it makes particular provision for dyslexic young people.

And much more input that is all described in the report.

One important point highlighted from the report is that 'Whilst there is a provision for a young person to have an appropriate adult with them during their interaction with the legal process, unless it is someone they know and trust, they are unlikely to disclose their literacy difficulties. If this appropriate adult is also their parent, then there is the possibility that they might also have a difficulty with literacy'

Conclusively the project adds weight to evidence that 'there is higher incidence of dyslexia among young offenders than in the general population' (BDA 2004).

And that appropriate screening assessments and intervention will help build self esteems and breaks the cycle of re-offending. Further work is in progress at Wetherby Secure College of Learning and analysis continues to establish the relationship between undiagnosed dyslexia and young offending.

I would be inclined to appoint a person who has dyslexia, and has dealt with their condition and is in a position to help them by empathising with their condition. I would certainly will to help as this is my pet subject and I feel that I can communicate well.

Judging by the evidence collected so far and examining the behavioural aspect of dyslexia, I was forced to ask myself the question. What would have happened if I had different parents, and lived in a different social environment like some of my less fortunate school colleagues? Judging by the fact that I was socially isolated at school, my dyslexia not recognised and bullied by teachers at times.

LIFE IN A JAR

LIVING WITH DYSLEXIA

ON REFLECTION

I must say dyslexia has left its mark. As I reflect back on my turbulent past, and attempt to make sense of it. The pieces of the jigsaw began to fit together. The more answers about my condition provided me with a clearer picture. Those school days of being misunderstood and bullied into working, when I failed to understand the concept of plurals, nouns and dividing the words into their relevant syllables. When I was at home ill, I would look at comics and analyse the pictures in order to make sense of the words this seemed logical to be, and it was my way of formulating my own strategies in order to learn to read and write. I found that I was able to memorise words in their entirety and relay them whenever necessary, whenever I was tested. This became my saving grace and much was achieved by this method. In my mind to comprehend the English language depended on a number of factors, namely observation, listening to the sounds of words, and an interesting story to follow providing pictures to illustrate the main points. By the very power of the imagination the mind is capable of conjuring up a picture, that makes sense to the individual.

Another problem emerged from reflecting back to my past, I was suffering from light sensitivity and found that white paper with black print tended to cause problems. Often the words would merge and cause confusion. After hearing Bills story this problem began to make sense to me, I already wore reactor light glasses and placing yellow clear plastic onto white paper with black print made life much easier. As a result, I suffer from fewer headaches, and less fatigue, as I don't need to concentrate so much. Further more since I have received counselling, I have discovered my true self, my potential, and was able to look back at my dyslexic ridden past and grasp the fundamental problems that this disability provided. It is logically and understandably clear that the past cannot be rewritten, and perhaps in some cases there is a reason for experiencing such things. One reason may be in order for me to help other dyslexics, with the same or similar disabilities or to learn to survive in this harsh world, by developing a need to exist regardless of my disability. Whatever the reason, my own determination brought me to where I am today and although I have a lot of people to thank, who endeavoured to support me, my own strength of mind and courage of heart forced me forward into success.

I have my own faults as does many people no one is perfect, clumsiness is one of them, forgetfulness is another. But I try to compensate for these by using a pad and pen for short-term memory problems and a spell check, when writing reports. As a nurse my concentration and powers of observation need to be good, therefore I work on disciplining my mind and thinking about the planning stage of my job. Time management is one area that I am continuous of prioritising is another area of self-awareness in order to complete my tasks and become an efficient nurse.

My mother tells me 'Your father would be proud of you, in what you have achieved 'I Feel good knowing this, that at last I have succeeded in pleasing him that in itself is an achievement to reach his level of approval, my children will not need to try as hard for I firmly believe that you achieve to your own ability and ultimately please yourself, I would be proud of my children if they became whoever they wanted to be.

Four of my children are showing fine progress at school, but I will not allow them to mock any child who is struggling. After all that was it and me once could well be one of my grand children in the future. I help in class at my son Michael and Daniels school listening to children reading books and words. Also helping them to create things from materials in class, there is no pressure on them to learn they go at their own pace. The teachers do not allow children to get stressed and encourage them with praise and reward. Since this time my daughter Gemma has been to university and graduated with a degree in nursing, my daughter Jeni is a teaching assistant, Michael is a computer wiz another one graduated at university and Daniel is presently at university studying animation and gaming.

Personally, I still hate reading aloud, in public I get so confused. I spend a long time reading and have to rest between pages. Maps are a nightmare to read, and mobile phone numbers are dreadful to dial. I get numbers mixed up back to front especially 6 and 9, getting numbers backwards 12 becomes 21. I still have trouble with times tables and mix up dates and times of appointments. Messages are a problem I have to write them down immediately, and put reminders on post dates everywhere. Sylvia Moody's book 'Dyslexia in the work place' is very useful in getting me organised in my work place.

So, what about my future? This is never set out in stone I try to plan for the future but things change all the time, even when I wrote this book, I spent almost two years at Manchester University on a nursing course in connection with Mental health nursing. I passed all my assignments but one which was a research critique, I almost passed it but never quite hit the mark. I passed all my placements and portfolio and had a job waiting for me pending my results.

Then I was kicked off the course and had to seek work immediately, fortunately my old employer took me back. My biggest criticism of that University was that I felt unsupported by the tutors, this shows that even today people fail to know enough about dyslexia and go on teaching in ignorance.

I can only hope that one-day my campaigning for more support for dyslexics in all environments eventually gets through to the right people and help is in abundance. I am hoping that this book reaches the right people and helps to educate them into becoming active in the cause of helping others in the world.

I have now spent years as a qualified nurse both in the hospital and the private setting, I have also continued to enjoy my artwork both drawing and painting. Thanks to Miss Caines I have published five books of poetry and I am gathering a name for myself in the world of poetry. Thanks to Miss Kilby I have also written a number of novels under my name and pseudo names like 'The eight skulls of Teversham', 'The adventures of the time witches' The Cursed' 'Cracked porcelain' and many more.

My mother Rita Francis Sutton

LIFE IN A JAR

ACKNOWLEDEMENTS

I wish to thank so many people for being involved in my life and making this book possible. Starting with my parents my late father Leonard James Sutton and my dear supportive mother Rita Francis Sutton. To my dear long suffering wife Jayne for her support and understanding.

To my in laws Jim and Cynthia Clift, who is a tower of strength to us?

My children, Gemma, Jennifer (who is in the jar on the front cover of this book), Michael and Daniel.

Thank you to aunty Penny who taught me how to tell the time and who boosted my confidence. To my very good friend Richard Howarth, who helped me survive my school days? To Dorothea Goodwin who was like an aunty to me.

To Geoffrey Kay who is a friend Godfather to my son Daniel.

To Jennifer Sutherland who was a good childhood friend and neighbour.

To Jack and Betty Montgomery for helping me through hard times and providing me with nice holidays. To Anja and Ulf my friends in Sweden.

To all my long-suffering employers and past colleagues who have witnessed my mishaps with no explanation until now.

To all those friends and colleagues at Trough house who have been very supportive. And to anyone else who I may have missed in my effort to remember so many people involved in my life.

LOVE TO YOU ALL

My father Leonard James Sutton

LIFE IN A JAR

LIVING WITH DYSLEXIA

USEFUL ARTICLES
AND ADDRESSES

BBC education (2004) Trendy teaching was 'crackers' David Bell

Website http://news.bbcco.uk/1/hi/education/3716518.stm

Brightstar (2004) how does brightstar work?

Brightstar London- SE Centre

Brightstar dyslexic centre, Friars house, 157-168 Black friars road,

London SE 1 8EZ

0870 3000 777

British Dyslexia Association B.D.A (2004) Unrecognised dyslexia and the route to offending

British Dyslexia Association

98, London road,

Reading RG1 5AU

0118966 2677

Dyslexic help line 01352 716656

Dyslexia Kidshealth website Nemours foundation

Dyslexic research trust (2004). http://www.dyslexic.org.uk/aboutdyslexia.htm

65 Kingston road

Oxford OX2 6RJ

01865 552303

'Go phonics' Multi-sensory phonics program USA

Foundations for learning, LLC

PMB 144 246 West Manson HWY, Chelan WA 98816

International dyslexia association

Chester building suite 382

8600 Lasalle road

Baltimore

Maryland 21286 –2044 USA

Professor Eric Wertelak . Welcome to dyslexia

Macalester college

Bristol dyslexia centre

10, Upper belgrave road

Clifton

Bristol BS8 2XH

0117 9739405

SKILL

National bureau for students with disabilities

Information service

Chapter house

18-20 Crucifix lane

London SE1 3JW

0800 328 5050

Maple Hayes school

Abnalls Lane

Lichfield

Staffs WS13 8BL

01543-264387

Davis dyslexia association UK

Unit 3D

Staney place

Headcorn road

Staplehurst

Kent TN12 ODT

0870 443 9059

Ellis AW (1993) Reading, writing and dyslexia

Hornby (1984) Overcoming dyslexia, a straight forward guide for families and teachers. Martin Dunita LTD, London.

Thomson (1990) Evaluating teaching programs for children with specific learning difficulties. In Pumfrey and Elliot (Eds) Childrens difficulties in reading, spelling and writing. Falmer press London 316p

Davis, Ronald (1997) The gift of dyslexia

Bartlett D, Moody S (2000) Dyslexia in the work place

Whurr publishers London and Philadelphia

Kirby A (1999) Dyspraxia The hidden handicap

Condor book souvenir press (E&A) Ltd London

LDA

Abbeygate house

East road

Cambridge

0845 120 4776 <u>www.LDAlearning.com</u> Primary and special needs products

There are many more places to contact that can be located through any of the articles or addresses.

THE FUTURE

The future for me (the jar) is to make the jar known to as many people as possible. It is my ultimate desire to organise an exhibition of art and literature called 'LIFE IN A JAR' with work from people all over England. This would involve any sort of art work and literature in conjunction with people's interpretations of Life in a jar.

The idea is to raise awareness to various disabilities and promote support in charitable organisations. It is my goal to achieve this project within the next few years, and form a chain reaction around the world, with exhibitions all over the world. Of course, an international exhibition would prove even more fruitful and rewarding to many people, so many gifted people could be recognised through their work. Life in a jar is not a dream it's a reality.

Stephen Sutton 'The jar'

steversutton@hotmail.co.uk

MY POETRY (https://www.facebook.com/ groups/500590300767430)

LIFE IN A JAR

This is a prison of life's long pain
As for the meaning let me explain
People suffer from anxiety and fame
Some are blind, deaf and some are lame
Without all these things they would go very far
Until this time they must live in a jar

Fame restricts you from the freedom to move
Make plans for the future that they disapprove
A clear direct guided by fools around
Controlled like a robot without any sound
You live every day in a jar
A lost identity you don't know who you are

The title is ambiguous as you can see
But it expresses all things to me
Whether you are ill or just a star
Just remember you live in a jar
Who said your world is an oyster expression like that
Must have been crazy or some sort of Pratt

ACTION HERO

I want to be an action hero
So I can stop kids bullying me
Brave like an action hero
And walk around totally free

In my dreams I am an action hero
Fighting my way through school
Walking around like an action hero
Instead of somebody's fool

I want to be an action hero
Playing in the school yard
Fighting off all the bullies
Making out to be hard

My life in school at present
Is being pushed against the wall
But my life as an action hero
I have the power to conquer all

LIFES FIRST BREATH

Echoes of laughter
Or cups of joy
The beginning of life
For a girl or a boy
A wonderful moment
You can clearly see
From the very start
Of wonders to be
From life's first breath
Or the first beat of the heart
With close companions
Who will never depart?
For trial and error
Will teach us the way
Learn from our mistakes
From day to day

MY BEST FRIEND

IN MEMORY OF RICHARD HOWARTH

In times of need
You came to me
A friend of mine
You will ever be

In school days
We worked and played
We lived our lives
And never strayed

Listening to music
Of the day
Sharing experiences
In our own special way

We grew up
And lived our own lives
Both moved away
And married our wives

We both had children
Our own family home
Giving up freedom
Nowhere to roam

In time we reconnected
Together again
Years have passed by us
But were still the same

Supporting each other
By text or by phone
Just letter us know
That were not alone

NOBODY LISTENS

by Stephen Robert Sutton

Nobody listens
Nobody cares
Nobody wants to
Nobody dares

Frightened to speak
Left on the shelf
No one understands
My mental health

Vicious and spiteful
Echoes remain
No one is listening
To those insane

I speak of my illness
My problems in life
You cannot see madness
Not without strife

The darkness is present
The demons appear
You cannot see them
But believe me they're here

Nobody listens
To the words that I say
They think I am sane
But I muddle through the day

One day they will listen
And remember my name
Find my poor body
And say what a shame

Nobody listens
Nobody cares
Nobody wants to
Nobody dares

DO YOU SEE ME?

by Stephen Robert Sutton

Do you see me?
Do you care?
Am I invisible?
Just in the air

Do you see through me?
Like a ghost in the night
So do I scare you?
Fill you with fright

You walk right past me
Like I am not there
With no acknowledgement
Like you don't even care

You see only my fault
Like a lantern alight
Showing my madness
The goods not in sight

I look in a mirror
And I see my reflection
Is it really me?
Or just a deception

I want to scream
Just to be seen
Or trash everywhere
Just to be seen

Do you see me?
Could you just care?
Just speak to me
Make me aware

ALL LIVES MATTER

by Stephen Robert Sutton

Black lives matter
We know this is true
When we are caged in
Like animals in a zoo

Frustrated by our system
That is the case
Living like slaves
In our human race

But every life matters
All colour and creed
Don't live like the rich folk
Governed by greed

Live life in harmony
Do what is best
Share all your love
And damn all the rest

Freedom is important
With no slavery
Fighting for justice
Live in harmony

STEPHEN SUTTON

DEEP *in* THOUGHT

MORE POEMS
FROM THE JAR

EIGHT SKULLS OF
TEVERSHAM

ORIGIN OF THE WITCHES

SB SUTTON